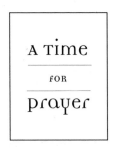

A Time
———
FOR
———
prayer

Volumes in the Pathway to the Heart of God series

PATHWAY TO THE HEART OF GOD

A Time
for
prayer

TERRY W. GLASPEY

Cumberland House Publishing
Nashville, Tennessee

Published by Cumberland House Publishing, Inc., 431 Hard-
ing Industrial Drive, Nashville, Tennessee 37211

Unless otherwise indicated, verses are taken from the Holy
Bible, New International Version ®, Copyright © 1973, 1978,
1984 by the International Bible Society. Used by permission
of Zondervan Publishing House. The "NIV" and "New International Version" trademarks are registered in the United
States Patent and Trademark Office by the International
Bible Society.

Cover design by Karen Phillips
Text design by Julia M. Pitkin

Library of Congress Cataloging-in-Publication Data

Glaspey, Terry W.
    A time for prayer / Terry W. Glaspey
        p. cm. -- (Pathway to the heart of God series)
    ISBN 1-58182-131-X (hardcover)
    1. Prayer--Christianity. I. Title.

    BV210.2 .G59 2000
    248.3'2--dc21   00-057066
Printed in the United States of America
1 2 3 4 5 6 7 8 — 05 04 03 02 01 00

contents

introduction

What is prayer?

If asked that question, most of us would be able to give some sort of answer. But likely, in the very process of responding, we would realize that our answer was not quite as satisfying as we'd like it to be. I suppose that we all think we know what prayer is, but when we reflect just a bit deeper, we realize there is much about it we don't know or understand—that it is something of a mystery.

That shouldn't be too surprising. After all, the topic of prayer touches the intersection of the natural and the supernatural, for prayer is a point of connection between the human and the Divine, between earth and heaven.

At its heart, prayer is personal communication with a loving God. It is the way we reach out to our Creator. Prayer arises within us not only from a proper sense of our duty to Him (the One to whom we owe our very existence), but also because it is the natural response of a heart and life touched by His love and grace. Prayer is powerful because God hears us and responds to the deepest cries of our souls.

This little book you hold in your hand is the first of four little books about prayer. This particular volume will focus on looking at what prayer really is and at how God uses it so powerfully in our lives. The other books in the series will examine the different elements of a balanced prayer life *(The Joy of Prayer)*, wrestle with some tough questions about prayer *(The Journey of Prayer)*, and provide practical steps toward making prayer a more integral part of our lives *(The Experience of Prayer)*. Each of the four books is a part of the whole. Taken together, their goal is not only to help us understand prayer a little better, but also to inspire us to begin to pray.

Prayer is a topic that continues to be much discussed these days, especially by those who are concerned with making sense of their spiritual lives. There are lots of books around that attempt to explain the ins and outs of what prayer is and how it affects one's life. Some of them claim to have all the answers, to have unlocked some secret key or system for making prayer effective for the reader.

I make no such claim. Like you, I am a learner in the school of prayer. But one of the important things I have learned is that I am not on my own when it comes to making sense of this crucial element of my spiritual life. Many great thinkers, writers, theologians, mystics, and activists have ruminated deeply on this important topic. In this book, I hope to share a little of what I've learned from them, mostly in their own words. If, like me, you realize you have a lot to learn and you truly desire to make your prayer life more meaningful, then I invite you to join me in meditating on some of the most profound and life-changing words ever written about prayer.

Each year brings a multitude of new books on prayer. One of the lessons I have learned about such books is that the most recent ones are not necessarily the best ones. It seems that a lot of books published these days are tainted with our modern materialistic values or our current obsession with the therapeutic sphere. Such books tend to be more concerned with using prayer as a way to get what we want or as a method for obtaining inner peace and tranquility than with learning how to make communication with God a part of our honest everyday existence and with growing into a more intimate relationship with Him.

I invite you, then, to join me on a journey that will sample the thoughts of some of the most insightful Christian believers who ever lived (along with a handful of others who thought deeply about the subject). These nuggets of wisdom are best absorbed thoughtfully and slowly, a few at a time. If we are to enter the school of prayer, we must not rush to consider ourselves graduates. Savor these thoughts. Meditate on them. Argue with them. Make them your own.

The writers quoted in this book come from a variety of time periods, religious traditions, cultures, and life experiences. Be forewarned: They do not always agree with each other. Most of the time I have simply allowed their disagreements to stand, expecting the reader to ponder their thoughts with discernment and draw his or her own conclusions. At other times, I have tried to synthesize the various insights together, still endeavoring to avoid the temptation of superficially explaining away the mysteries that will always surround this topic.

Sprinkled in with the text you'll also find some

of my favorite prayers from classic writers, many of them composed by the same writers whose thoughts on prayer we will consider. You can use these prayers as models to fashion your own, as inspiration to prepare your heart to pray, or as a way to give voice to concerns and feelings you cannot articulate as well as these saints. You and I can make these prayers our own, for often they can help us express what we would struggle to put into words for ourselves. When prayed with focus and concentration, they can give our hearts wings to fly upward to God.

Finally, I have concluded each section of this book with a prayer I have written. These little prayers are attempts to put the truths of the chapter into practice, for it does us little good to think about prayer or read about praying if we don't actually pray.

I hope you will find this little book to be a helpful companion as you travel your own spiritual path. Think of it as a map you can use as you begin your personal journey into God's heart.

Terry W. Glaspey

A Time

FOR

prayer

–I–
WHAT IS PRAYER?

few questions are as important as this one.

To ask the question, "What is prayer?" is to ask a question of such depth that it is beyond our limited human understanding to ever fully answer. The question probes not only the mysteries of what it means to be a human being, but even inquires into the mystery of God Himself. If we were to spend our entire lives and our complete hearts in the attempt to understand what prayer is and how to pray more effectively, we could never exhaust from this subject what there is to learn.

Because it is a topic too deep for the human intellect, it requires that we look to God as our teacher. As one early church theologian wrote:

> *The discussion of prayer is so great*
> *that it requires the Father to reveal it,*
> *his firstborn Word to teach it, and the Spirit*
> *to enable us to think and speak*
> *rightly of so great a subject.*
> —ORIGEN

Nevertheless, throughout history, great men and women have been bold to reflect on the meaning of prayer, looking to the Scriptures and their own experiences with God. These saints have provided us with many helpful insights into this God-instituted action that weds our earthly lives to the heavenly realm.

The starting point of any study is found in careful definition. With prayer, many definitions have been offered. Some of those we find in the classic Christian writings are theologically and philosophically profound, the result of careful reflection:

*Prayer is an offering up of our desires unto God,
for things agreeable to His will, in the name of Christ,
with confession of our sins, and thankful
acknowledgment of his mercies.*
—WESTMINSTER SHORTER CATECHISM

*The ancients ably defined prayer
as* Ascensus mentis ad Deum, *a
climbing up of the heart unto God.*
—MARTIN LUTHER

*God has instituted prayer so as to confer
upon his creatures the dignity of causality.*
—BLAISE PASCAL

*Prayer is conversation with the
Existent One who is exalted above the
world cycle, above the falsity and wrongness
in which the world is submerged.*
—NICHOLAS BERDYAEV

"Why has God established prayer?"
asks Pascal. And Pascal's first answer
to his own great Question is this: God has
established prayer in the moral world
in order "to communicate to His creatures
the dignity of causality." That is to
say, to give us a touch and a taste
of what it is to be a Creator.
—ALEXANDER WHYTE

Prayer is one of the necessary wheels
of the machinery of providence.
—CHARLES SPURGEON

But these more philosophical definitions should never cause us to think of prayer merely as an abstract theological subject. For prayer is a practice, not an idea; an action, not an abstraction:

*Prayer is to religion what original research
is to science.*
—p.t. forsyth

Prayer is to religion what thinking is to philosophy.
—NOVALIS

Other definitions through the ages have focused on the practicality of prayer, demonstrating why it is so essential in the life of the believer:

*Prayer, in its simplest definition, is merely
a wish turned God-ward.*
—phillips brooks

*Prayer is a sincere, sensible, affectionate
pouring out of the soul to God, through Christ
in the strength and assistance of the Spirit,
for such things as God has promised.*
—JOHN BUNYAN

*Prayer is a right understanding
of that fullness of joy that is to come,
with well-longing and sure trust.*
—JULIAN OF NORWICH

*Prayer is simply a reverent, conscious
openness to God full of the desire to grow
in goodness and overcome evil.*
—FROM THE CLOUD OF UNKNOWING

For me, prayer means launching out
of the heart towards God; it means lifting
up one's eyes, quite simply, to Heaven, a cry
of grateful love from the crest of joy or the trough
of despair; it is a vast, supernatural force
which opens out my heart, and
binds me close to Jesus.
—THÉRÈSE DE LISIEUX

Prayer is the contact of a living soul with God.
In prayer, God stoops to kiss man, to bless man,
and to aid in everything that God can
devise or man can need.
—E.M. BOUNDS

Prayer is nought but a rising desire
of the heart into God by withdrawing
of the heart from all earthly thoughts.
—WALTER HILTON

*Prayer is to the spiritual life
what the beating of the pulse and the drawing
of the breath are to the life of the body.*
—JOHN HENRY NEWMAN

*Prayer is friendship with God.
Friendship is not merely a generalized mood:
every event is its occasion.*
—GEORGE BUTTRICK

*Prayer is the turning of
the mind and heart to God. To pray
is to stand in awareness before God,
to see him constantly and to talk
with him in hope and fear.*
—DEMETRIUS OF ROSTOV

*Where there is no prayer from the heart,
there is no religion.*
—AUGUSTE SABATIER

Of course, some definitions of prayer are merely humorous:

Prayers are little messages sent up to God at night to get a cheaper rate.
—A CHILD'S DEFINITION

Still other definitions are succinct and to the point. Any one of the following short definitions is packed with ample food for thought. Do not rush through them, but ponder them in your mind and savor them in your heart. See what they can teach us.

Prayer is conversation with God.
—CLEMENT OF ALEXANDRIA

*[Prayer is] an earnest and familiar
talking with God.*
—JOHN KNOX

*Prayer is the soul's breathing itself
into the bosom of its heavenly Father.*
—THOMAS WATSON

Prayer is the gymnasium of the soul.
—SAMUEL M. ZWEMER

Prayer is a time exposure of the soul to God.
—E. STANLEY JONES

Prayer is keeping company with God.
—CLEMENT OF ALEXANDRIA

To pray means willing to be naive.
—EMILIE GRIFFIN

Heart speaks to heart.
—JOHN HENRY NEWMAN

Some definitions are quite poetic, capturing in striking metaphors something of the mystery of prayer:

*Prayer is the wing wherewith
the soul flies to heaven and meditation
the eye wherewith we see God.*
—AMBROSE

Prayer is a fragrant dew,
but we must pray with a pure heart to
feel this dew. There flows from prayer a
delicious sweetness, like the juice of very ripe
grapes. Troubles melt away before a fervent
prayer like snow before the sun. To approach
God one should go straight to him, like a ball from
a cannon. Prayer disengages our soul from matter;
it raises it on high, like the fire that inflates a balloon.
The more we pray, the more we wish to pray. Like a
fish which at first swims on the surface of the water,
and afterwards plunges down and is always going
deeper, the soul plunges, dives, and loses itself in
the sweetness of conversing with God. Prayer
is the holy water that by its flow makes the
plants of our good desires grow green and
flourish, that cleanses our souls of their
imperfections, and that quenches the
thirst of passion in our hearts.
—JOHN VIANNEY

Prayer is like a volcano.
Its foundation lies in the silent depths.
Its culmination is in turbulent eruption.
Its final stage lies in a return to silence.
—DONALD BLOESCH

Prayer is the peace of our spirit,
the stillness of our thoughts, the evenness
of our recollection, the sea of our meditation, the
rest of our cares, and the calm of our tempest.
—JEREMY TAYLOR

To pray is to descend with the mind into
the heart, and there to stand before the face of the
Lord, ever present, all-seeing within you.
—THEOPHAN THE RECLUSE

To pray is to dream in league with God,
to envision His holy visions.
—ABRAHAM HESCHEL

It is not only the theologians and spiritual writers who have grappled with the meaning of prayer. Even the poets have mused on its mysteries.

Prayer is the world in tune,
A spirit-voice, And vocal joys,
Whose echo is heaven's bliss.
—HENRY VAUGHN

Prayer is the little implement
Through which Men reach
Where Presence—is denied them.
They fling their Speech
By means of it—in God's Ear—
If then He hear—
This sums the Apparatus
Comprised in Prayer.
—EMILY DICKINSON

And here, from George Herbert, is quite possibly the greatest poem about prayer:

Prayer, the Church's banquet, Angels' age,
God's breath in man returning to his birth,
The soul in paraphrase, heart in pilgrimage.
The Christian plummet sounding heaven and earth;
Engine against the Almighty, sinners' tower,
Reversed thunder, Christ-side-piercing spear,
The six-days world transposing in an hour,
A kind of tune, which all things hear and fear;
Softness, and peace, and joy, and love, and bliss,
Exalted manna, gladness of the best,
Heaven in ordinary, man well dressed,
The Milky Way, the bird of paradise,
Church-bells beyond the stars heard, the soul's blood,
The land of spices; something understood.
— GEORGE HERBERT

Carefully constructed theological statements,
brilliant metaphors and poems, and intense ecsta-
tic ejaculations of the heart: all these have been
pressed into service to define prayer. But none of
them even come near to exhausting the richness of
all that prayer is. Perhaps our efforts with language
are best used not in definition and explanation, but
in the simple act of praying. As P.T. Forsyth has so
well stated:

> *Prayer is the highest use to which*
> *speech can be put.*
> —P.T. FORSYTH

Most holy god,
no metaphor can contain,
nor definition encompass,
the greatness of the privilege you have so
graciously granted to us.
that we, the weak and unstable creature
should have such ready access to the ear
of the one who created us.
grant that we may we live up to the responsibility,
and glory in the prerogative we have
as sons and daughters of a loving father.
in jesus' name.
amen.

THE NECESSITY OF PRAYER

It is usually not very hard for others to convince us to spend time on things that we deem to be truly important. We rarely need, for example, to be lectured on the necessity of eating or sleeping. But some things we know to be important are not as easy to convince ourselves to do, such as getting adequate exercise. We struggle to find the time to work out, even though we know that our bodies need regular exertion if our health is to be maintained.

Prayer is as necessary to our spiritual health as exercise is to our bodily health. But still we seem to need to be constantly reminded. Sometimes preachers will pause in the middle of a sermon and decry our modern prayerlessness by pointing to the "good old days" when Christians really knew how to pray. Certainly the lack of prayer among modern Christians is a scandal, but we are mistaken if we imagine that the lack of an active prayer life is a modern phenomenon. Throughout the history of the church, great writers on prayer have always found it necessary to remind believers of the importance of praying.

It is all too easy for us, just as it was for believers in earlier centuries, to get so caught up in the busyness of our lives that we neglect the important duty and privilege of prayer. For to pray well demands effort and concentration, the focusing of our desires, and the commitment of our time. But, as the great saints remind us, what could be more deserving of the effort it requires?

*The present congregations need
instruction not on how to pray but on the
necessity of prayer to begin with.*
—GREGORY OF NYSSA

*I have come to the conclusion
that the vast majority of Christians
do not pray at all.*
—J.C. RYLE

To pray rightly is a rare gift.
—JOHN CALVIN

*As it is the business of tailors
to make clothes and of cobblers to
mend shoes, so it is the business
of Christians to pray.*
—MARTIN LUTHER

Prayer is the very life-breath of true Christianity.
—J.C. RYLE

The whole reason why we pray
is to be united into the vision and
contemplation of him to whom we pray.
—JULIAN OF NORWICH

Apostasy begins in the closet.
No man ever backslid from the life
and power of Christianity who continued
constant and fervent in private prayer.
He who prays without ceasing
is likely to rejoice evermore.
—ADAM CLARKE

*What is the reason that some believers
are so much brighter and holier than others?
I believe the difference, in nineteen cases out
of twenty, arises from different habits about
private prayer. I believe that those who are
not eminently holy pray little, and those
who are eminently holy pray much.*
—J.C. RYLE

An active life of prayer offers us the promise of
spiritual growth, holiness, and a deeper intimacy
with God. We must not think of it, however, as a
cure-all, an escape hatch from the troubles of life,
or a way to guarantee our personal happiness.
Instead, prayer is a work to which we must
commit ourselves if we are to make sense of our
lives in the light of eternity.

Prayer is no panacea,
no substitute for action. It is, rather,
like a beam thrown from a flashlight
before us into the darkness. It is in this
light that we who grope, stumble, and climb,
discover where we stand, what surrounds us,
and the course which we should choose. Prayer
makes visible the right, and reveals what is
hampering and false. In its radiance, we
behold the worth of our efforts, the
range of our hopes, and the
meaning of our deeds.
—ABRAHAM HESCHEL

Often, we are reminded of the importance of prayer by the realization that we have nowhere else to go. When we reach the end of our rope, have exerted ourselves to the fullest extent, and even felt tempted to simply give up, we are reminded that we are not alone, nor are we abandoned to our own resources. God is both caring and responsive, and He will meet with us in prayer.

The man who really prays never attempts to justify himself. In true prayer, he knows that he cannot do so.
—KARL BARTH

The best disposition for praying is that of being desolate, forsaken, stripped of everything.
—AUGUSTINE

I have been driven many times to my knees by the overwhelming conviction that I had nowhere else to go. My own wisdom, and that of all about me seemed insufficient for the day.
—ABRAHAM LINCOLN

True prayers are like those carrier pigeons which find their way so well; they cannot fail to go to heaven, for it is from heaven that they came; they are only going home.
—CHARLES SPURGEON

*Prayer is…a renunciation
of human means. It is not merely
the point beyond which I could not go,
the limit of my power which dissolves into
impotence, but it is indeed a stripping bare,
the abandonment of all human apparatus
in order to place myself, without arms or
equipment, into the hands of the
Lord, who decides and fulfills.*
—JACQUES ELLUL

Gracious heavenly father,
forgive us for so often losing sight
of the importance of prayer.
Awaken in us the realization that
you are our source of hope
And that you are always waiting for us
to place our needs in your hands.
Help us to learn to come to you regularly,
even when there is no crisis,
And not just at moments of discouragement
and desperation.
Teach us to see prayer from
a renewed perspective.
In Jesus' name,
Amen.

— 3 —

THE POWER OF PRAYER

A physician who has discovered the cure for a devastating disease would surely not hide the results of his research, would he? He wouldn't want to die with his secret unrevealed. Rather, wouldn't he be eager to share the fruit of his years of labor? Wouldn't he want to do everything in his power to let the human race know about his marvelous discovery, the secret to defeating the disease?

We are the beneficiaries of such a secret—a powerful, life-changing cure for the ills of the human race. That secret, of course, is prayer.

Perhaps because of the way we have been raised, or because of our own disappointing experiences with prayer, we do not see it for the powerful tool that it is. Prayer is not merely a religious nicety meant to be taken lightly, but a dangerous, earth-shattering act, the powerful engine that God uses to accomplish His will on this earth.

The very realization that God uses our seemingly feeble prayers to accomplish His will should fill us with awe and wonder. How astonishing that He chooses to use the prayers of His children to make things happen in both the earthly and the heavenly realms!

God shapes the world by prayer.
—E.M. BOUNDS

God does nothing but in answer to prayer.
—JOHN WESLEY

The archimedean point outside
the world is the little chamber where
a true suppliant prays in all sincerity—
where he lifts the world off its hinges.
—SÖREN KIERKEGAARD

Christians who pray are helpers and
saviors, yea masters and gods of the world.
They are the legs which bear the world.
—MARTIN LUTHER

Prayer moves the hand which moves the world.
—JOHN AIKMAN WALLACE

More things are wrought by prayer
Than this world dreams of.
Wherefore, let thy voice
Rise like a fountain for me
night and day.
For what are men better than
sheep or goats
That nourish a blind life
within the brain,
If knowing God, they lift not
hands of prayer
Both for themselves and
those who call them friends?
For so the whole round earth
is every way
Bound by gold chains about
the feet of God.
—ALFRED LORD TENNYSON

Through prayer, souls are brought into God's kingdom, lives changed, and miracles performed. It is almost too incredible to believe that God allows us to have a part in His work through this powerful tool, but it is true!

Prayer is an essential link in the chain of causes that lead to a revival, as much so as truth is. Some have zealously used truth to convert men, and laid very little stress on prayer. They have preached, and talked, and distributed tracts with great zeal, and then wondered that they had so little success. And the reason was, that they forgot to use the other branch of the means, effectual prayer. They overlooked the fact that truth by itself will never produce the effect, without the Spirit of God, and that the Spirit is given in answer to prayer.
—CHARLES G. FINNEY

*In prayer you align yourselves
to the purpose and power of God
and He is able to do things through you
that He couldn't do otherwise. For this is
an open universe, where some things are
left open, contingent upon our doing them.
If we do not do them, they will never be done.
For God has left certain things open
to prayer—things which will never
be done except as we pray.*
—E. STANLEY JONES

*Prayer has been known to recall
the souls of the departed from the very
path of death, to transform the weak, to
restore the sick, to purge the possessed, to open
prison-bars, to loose the bonds of the innocent.
Likewise it washes away faults, repels temptations,
extinguishes persecutions, consoles the fainthearted,
cheers the high-spirited, escorts travelers, appeases
waves, makes robbers stand aghast, nourishes
the poor, governs the rich, upraises the fallen,
arrests the falling, confirms the standing.*
—TERTULLIAN

Heavenly father,
we so often fail to recognize the power
you have entrusted to us,
The privilege we so little deserve.
give us, father, the courage
and wisdom to use this gift
To bring healing and comfort to the lives of others,
To bring strength to our own lives,
And to bring us ever closer to you.
In Jesus' name,
Amen.

-4-

GOD ANSWERS PRAYER

If we fail to see the power of prayer and perceive of it only as a meaningless devotional exercise, we will always ask in our hearts: "Why pray?" Are we just fooling ourselves? Just going through the motions? Trying to prove something to ourselves?

If our prayers are not answered, then perhaps we are deceiving ourselves. Is God real to us, or is He not? If God is not real to us, then how can our prayers be answered? When He is not real to us, in our own hearts we realize we are not praying because in our heart of hearts we are unsure if there is anyone to hear our prayers.

But there is a God who lives and whose ears are opened to us. Because He is not just a philosophical concept or a metaphysical force, we have the promise that our prayers are heard and answered. God has revealed Himself to be a personal, infinite God, one who deeply loves His children and desires the best for them.

Prayer, then, is not just a form of inspirational self-talk or an empty religious ritual. The God who created and controls all that is in the universe has shown that He will move His hand in answer to our requests.

Then you will call upon
me and come and pray to me,
and I will listen to you.
—JEREMIAH 29:12

0 people of Zion,
who live in Jerusalem,
you will weep no more. How
gracious he will be when you cry
for help! As soon as he hears,
he will answer you.
—ISAIAH 30:19

For everyone who asks receives;
he who seeks finds; and to him who
knocks, the door will be opened.
—MATTHEW 7:8

*Until now you have not
asked for anything in my name.
Ask and you will receive, and
your joy will be complete.*
—JOHN 16:24

*We must not conceive of prayer as an
overcoming of God's reluctance, but as a
laying hold of His highest willingness.*
—R.C. TRENCH

*Praying is dangerous business.
Results do come.*
—G. CHRISTIE SWAIN

*Pray the largest prayers.
You cannot think a prayer so large
that God, in answering it, will not wish
you had made it larger. Pray not
for crutches but for wings!*
—PHILLIPS BROOKS

*Let this be the first and most important
point, that all our prayers must be based and
rest upon obedience to God, irrespective of our
person, whether we be sinners or saints, worthy
or unworthy. And we must know that God will
not have it treated as a jest, but be angry, and
punish all who do not pray, as surely as He
punishes all other disobedience; next, that He will
not suffer our prayers to be in vain or lost. For if He
did not intend to answer your prayer, He would not
bid you pray and add such a severe commandment
to it. In the second place, we should be the more
urged and incited to pray because God has also
added a promise, and declared that it shall surely be
done to us as we pray, as He says in Psalm 50:15:
"Call upon Me in the day of trouble: I will deliver
thee." And Christ in the Gospel of St. Matthew,
7:7: "Ask, and it shall be given you. For every one
that asketh receiveth." Such promises ought certainly
to encourage and kindle our hearts to pray with
pleasure and delight, since He testifies with
His [own] word that our prayer is heartily
pleasing to Him, moreover, that it shall
assuredly be heard and granted, in order
that we may not despise it or think
lightly of it, and pray at a venture.*
—MARTIN LUTHER

We do not pray for the sake
of praying, but for the sake of being heard.
We do not pray in order to listen to ourselves
praying but in order that God may hear us
and answer us. Also, we do not pray
in order to receive just any answer:
it must be God's answer.
—THOMAS MERTON

Prayer is the slender sinew that
moves the muscle of omnipotence.
—J. EDWIN HARTILL

When we shoot an arrow, we look
to the fall of it; when we send a ship to sea,
we look for the return of it; and when we sow seed,
we look for a harvest, and so when we sow
our prayers into God's bosom, shall
we not look for an answer?
—RICHARD SIBBES

I live in the spirit of prayer.
I pray as I walk about, when
I lie down and when I rise up.
And the answers are always coming.
—GEORGE MUELLER

If your troubles are deep-seated
or long-standing, try kneeling.
—UNKNOWN

When I pray coincidences happen,
and when I do not, they don't.
—WILLIAM TEMPLE

The firmament of the Bible is ablaze
with answers to prayer.
—T.L. CUYLER

Sometimes our prayers, though, can become merely a pretense while we find alternate ways to get what we want.

Next week it would be Bobby's birthday. He had clearly in mind what he hoped to get as gifts. After saying his prayers at night, he raised his voice and prayed very loudly: "Dear God, I pray that I will get a new bicycle and an electric train for my birthday. Amen." "Why are you praying so loudly?" asked his brother. "God isn't deaf." "I know," replied Bobby, "But Grandma is."

—UNKNOWN

Some people treat God
as they do a lawyer, they go to Him
only when they are in trouble.
—UNKNOWN

What is the use of praying
if at the very moment of prayer,
we have so little confidence in God
that we are busy planning our own
kind of answer to our prayer?
—THOMAS MERTON

What is it but blasphemy
when God is merely my means to an end?
That takes its toll. If we turn God into a puppet
of our own desires—even when that happens by
the pious route of prayer—then He shuts up His
heaven and we find ourselves thrown back
into the silence of our unredeemed life.
—HELMUT THIELICKE

Let us never forget that we do not receive answers to our prayers because we use the "proper formula," because God is awed with our faith, or because we deserve an answer. Our prayers are answered because God delights in answering them. Before God our prayers are as valuable as those of the most holy of the saints.

Therefore you should say:
My prayer is as precious, holy and
pleasing to God as that of St. Paul or of
the most holy saints.…God does not regard
prayer on account of the person, but on account
of His word and obedience thereto. For on the
commandment on which all the saints rest their
prayer I, too, rest mine. Moreover I pray for the
same thing for which they all pray and ever
have prayed; besides, I have just as great
a need of it as those great saints.
—MARTIN LUTHER

And, of course, the greatest answer to our prayers is God Himself because He is our greatest need.

*What if the main object in God's
idea of prayer be the supplying of
our great, our endless need—the need of
Himself? What if the good of all our smaller
and lower needs lies in this, that they help to
drive us to God? Hunger may drive the runaway
child home, and he may or may not be fed at once,
but he needs his mother more than his dinner.
Communion with God is the one need of the soul
beyond all other need, prayer is the beginning
of that communion, and some need is the
motive of that prayer. Our wants are for the
sake of our coming into communion
with God, our eternal need.*
—GEORGE MACDONALD

Lord,
we confess our timidity before you,
which causes us to shy away from
asking you to meet our needs.
we confess our false sense of decorum,
which makes us believe that it is unseemly
to pour our heart out to you.
we confess our lack of faith,
which makes us doubt your goodness and power.
Lord, we believe you desire to answer our prayers.
Help us in our unbelief
Amen.

-5-

PRAYER: A DUTY
AND A DISCIPLINE

Despite the fact that we realize the importance and power of prayer, the reality is that most of us spend very little time praying.

Many of us are "functional atheists." We say all the right words, but there is little evidence of our belief having much meaning when it comes to the way we live our lives. We say that God is aware of our predicaments, that He is able to help us in every situation, and that He is willing to come to our aid. But though we mouth these fine sentiments, what is our response in the moment of our deepest need? Is our first thought to go to Him, or is it to strive and manipulate and work out our own solutions to our problems?

When it comes to the way we actually live our lives, what we really believe about God becomes painfully obvious. Often, in the moment of crisis, the last thing we think to do is to pray.

What this reveals about us is that we are not truly convinced of our own convictions. We have failed to grasp the eternal significance of prayer.

*The little estimate we put on prayer is evident
from the little time we give to it.*
—E.M. BOUNDS

The worst sin is prayerlessness.
—P.T. FORSYTH

The chief failure in prayer is its cessation.
—DONALD BLOESCH

*As for me, far be it from me that I should
sin against the LORD by failing to pray for you*
—I SAMUEL 12:23

Perhaps our excuse is that we are too busy, that the multiplying demands of our lives do not leave us with sufficient time to give to prayer. Such a rationalization would not have convinced the great Christian writers.

If you are too busy to pray,
then you are too busy.
—W.E. SANGSTER

Every Christian needs a
half hour of prayer each day,
except when he is busy,
then he needs an hour.
—FRANCIS DE SALES

I have so much business
I cannot get on without spending
three hours daily in prayer.
—MARTIN LUTHER

The truth is, many of us wait to feel inspired or spiritually at peace before we are ready to pray. We forget that it is when we are off-balance, confused, frustrated, angry, disappointed, or under temptation that we most need to seek God's presence.

If we wait until we feel like praying, our praying will be as sporadic and undependable as our emotional states. We must commit ourselves to regular prayer, even when our emotions are reluctant to come along for the ride.

If you can't pray—at least say your prayers.
—GEORGES BERNANOS

You will never aspire to pray
unless you urge and force yourselves.
—JOHN CALVIN

To learn to pray with freedom,
force yourself to pray.
—P.T. FORSYTH

Then Jesus told his disciples a
parable to show them that they should
always pray and not give up.
—LUKE 18:1

Or perhaps, if we are honest, we realize that our
reluctance comes from the fact that prayer—true
prayer—demands effort.

Do not work so hard for Christ
that you have no strength to pray,
for prayer requires strength.
—J. HUDSON TAYLOR

To pray is to work.
—BENEDICTINE MOTTO

But we must realize that for the Christian, prayer is not an optional activity. It is not just one of many items on the smorgasbord of religious actions that we can choose to perform. Instead, it is the duty of every true believer to pray.

*Be joyful in hope, patient in
affliction, faithful in prayer.*
—ROMANS 12:12

*Devote yourselves to prayer,
being watchful and thankful.*
—COLOSSIANS 4:2

It is our duty and obligation
to pray if we would be Christians,
as much as it is our duty and obligation
to obey our parents and the government,
for by calling upon it and praying the name
of God is honored and profitably employed.
This you must note above all things, that thereby
you may silence and repel such thoughts as would
keep and deter us from prayer. For just as it would
be idle for a son to say to his father, "Of what
advantage is my obedience? I will go and do
what I can; it is all the same," but there stands
the commandment, Thou shalt and must
do it, so also here it is not left to my will
to do it or leave it undone, but prayer
shall and must be offered at the risk
of God's wrath and displeasure.
—MARTIN LUTHER

*I want men everywhere
to lift up holy hands in prayer,
without anger or disputing.*
—1 TIMOTHY 2:8

*Perhaps little praying is worse
than no praying. Little praying is a
kind of make-believe, a salve for the
conscience, a farce and a delusion.*
—E.M. BOUNDS

*So when Christ commands us to
pray, he does not leave it as a thing
of our own choice, but binds us to the
performance of it, for prayer is not only
required as a thing supplying our need—
for when we feel want, we need not be
provoked to prayer…but it is required as
a part of God's service. Anna being in
the temple, "served God by prayer."
By prayer the Apostles performed
that service to the Lord.*
—LANCELOT ANDREWES

If, then, our prayer is a duty to which we are called, and one which is not dependent upon our moods and feelings, we must find a way to carve out time in our day for this essential communication with God. It must become a habit.

The truth is that we only learn to pray
all the time everywhere after we have resolutely
set about praying some of the time somewhere.
—JOHN DALRYMPLE

Which forms of prayer are best?
There is no rule of thumb, for the reason
that every thumbprint is different and distinct.
Some habit of prayer is clearly wise, for all life
is built on habit, but the habit should be
under frequent scrutiny lest it harden
into a confining shell.
—GEORGE BUTTRICK

*One thing is certain, namely that
I daily ask with all my heart that you
have all the recollection and faithfulness to
God's Holy Spirit which you need to conquer
the difficulties of your position. For you have much
to fear both from within and without. From without,
the world smiles on you, and that side of the world
which is most adapted to you flatters your pride,
fosters it by all the considerations that you hold
at court. Then within you, you have to conquer
your taste for a refined life, your haughty,
disdainful temperament, and long-formed
habit of dissipation. The real remedy for
so many difficulties is to match, in spite
of everything that hinders you, some
fixed hour for prayer and reading.*
—FRANÇOIS FÉNELON

*It is an old custom of
the servants of God to have some
little prayers ready and to be frequently
darting them up to heaven during the day,
lifting their minds to God out of the mire of
this world. He who adopts this plan will
get great fruits with little pains.*
—PHILIP NERI

*The best help in all action
is to pray; that is true genius;
then one never goes wrong.*
—SÖREN KIERKEGAARD

*Aspire to God with short
but frequent outpourings of the heart;
admire His bounty; invoke His aid;
cast yourself in spirit at the foot of His
cross; adore His goodness; treat with
Him for your salvation; give Him your
whole soul a thousand times a day.*
—FRANCIS DE SALES

Of course it is a sad reflection upon our spiritual condition that we would ever have to be reminded of our duty to pray. If prayer is the natural outflow of our relationship with God, it should be among our greatest joys. It is to this that we will look in the next chapter.

*The disquieting thing is not simply
that we skimp and begrudge the duty
of prayer. The really disquieting thing is
that it should have to be numbered among
the duties at all. For we believe that we were
created "to glorify God and enjoy him forever."
And if the few, the very few, minutes we now
spend on intercourse with God are a burden
to us rather than a delight, what then?…
If we were perfected, prayer would not
be a duty, it would be a delight.*

—C.S. LEWIS

Heavenly Father,
There is a part of us that knows
we need to pray,
A part of us that cries out for the fulfillment
of our relationship with you.
There is also a part of us that is lazy,
confused, and faithless,
A part of us that cannot really accept
the truth about you.
Remind us Lord, that the basis of our faith
is not found in feelings, spiritual ecstasies,
nor clever spiritual technologies,
But in obedience to your calling.
And you have called us to pray.
Amen.

PRAYER:
A DIALOGUE AND
A DELIGHT

As C.S. Lewis indicated in the quote that closed the last chapter, prayer is not only a duty; it should be a delight as well. Why? Because true prayer is the greatest act of intimacy we have with a loving God.

Prayer is not a philosophical monologue or some kind of self-talk by which we work out our problems. Nor is it a religious exercise we perform in order to "gain points" or favor with God. It is not an address to an unknowable and impersonal Creator-Being, but communion with a loving heavenly Father. That is the great message of the Lord's Prayer.

The words "Our Father"
tell us: You have to deal not merely
with "the Divine"; not merely with a
mysterious, all-pervading Deity, but with
a Being; not merely with a Something, but
with a Someone Whom you can address;
not merely with an Authority which
touches you but with a Countenance
which you are called to look upon.
—ROMANO GUARDINI

When we call upon God, it is not in our own
strength, but through Jesus Christ, who has inter-
ceded with God on our behalf:

In him and through faith in
him [Christ] we may approach God
with freedom and confidence.
—EPHESIANS 3:12

He [Jesus Christ] is our mouth,
through which we speak to the Father;
He is our eye, through which we see the Father,
He is our right hand, through which we offer
ourselves to the Father. Unless He intercedes,
there is no intercession with God
either for us or for all saints.
—AMBROSE

Since we have a great high priest
who has gone through the heavens, Jesus
the Son of God, let us hold firmly to the faith
we profess. For we do not have a high priest who
is unable to sympathize with our weaknesses, but
we have one who has been tempted in every way,
just as we are—yet was without sin. Let us then
approach the throne of grace with confidence,
so that we may receive mercy and find
grace to help us in our time of need.
—HEBREWS 4:14-16

*Whenever believers prepare
themselves to pray to God, they
ought…to feel that their prayers are
sprinkled by the blood of our Lord Jesus
Christ, in order to be pure and clean,
and to be received by God as a
sweet-smelling sacrifice.*
—JOHN CALVIN

It is the Father to whom we pray and the Son who is our advocate. But the power and promptings of prayer come through the Holy Spirit.

*Pray in the Spirit on all occasions
with all kinds of prayers and requests.*
—EPHESIANS 6:18

In the same way, the Spirit helps us in our weakness. We do not know what we ought to pray for, but the Spirit himself intercedes for us with groans that words cannot express. And he who searches our hearts knows the mind of the Spirit, because the Spirit intercedes for the saints in accordance with God's will.
—ROMANS 8:26

[The Spirit] searches the deep things of God, offers, prompts and suggests to us in our prayers those very things that are in God's heart, to grant the things we desire of Him, so that it often comes to pass that a poor creature is carried on to speak God's very heart to Himself, and then God cannot, and will not deny.
—THOMAS GOODWIN

*If the skeleton and outline of our prayers
be by habit, almost a form, let us strive that
the clothing and filling up of our prayers
be as far as possible of the Spirit.*
—J.C. RYLE

*It is the easiest thing in a hundred
to fall from power to form, but it is the
hardest thing of many to keep in the life,
spirit and power of any one duty, especially
prayer. It is such a work that a man* without
the help of the Spirit *cannot do so much as
pray once, much less continue without, in a
sweet praying frame, and in praying,
so to pray as to have his prayer
ascend unto the ears of the
Lord of the Sabbath.*
—JOHN BUNYAN

The real basis of true prayer is our love for God.
We pray not only because we have needs or
because we feel a sense of duty, but because our
love for God is such that we seek His presence in
prayer.

Love.

Love is the key to true prayer.

"Because he loves me," says the LORD,
"I will rescue him; I will protect him, for he
acknowledges my name. He will call upon me,
and I will answer him; I will be with him in
trouble, I will deliver him and honor him."
—PSALM 91:14,15

True, whole prayer is nothing but love.
—AUGUSTINE

*As soon as we are with God in faith
and in love, we are in prayer.*
—FRANÇOIS FÉNELON

*This way of prayer, this simple
relationship to our Lord, is so suited
for everyone; it is just as suited for the dull
and the ignorant as it is for the well-educated.
This prayer, this experience which begins so simply,
has as its end a totally abandoned love to the
Lord. Only one thing is required—Love.*
—MADAME GUYON

*Homesickness for God is
a mark of the life of prayer.*
—JAMES HOUSTON

We cease to pray to God
as soon as we cease to love Him,
as soon as we cease to thirst for His
perfections. The coldness of our love
is the silence of our hearts toward God.
Without this we may pronounce prayers,
but we do not pray; for what shall lead us
to meditate upon the laws of God if it be
not the love of Him who has made
these laws? Let our hearts be
full of love, then, and
they will pray.
—FRANÇOIS FÉNELON

This kind of prayer, birthed in true relationship with God, is the kind of prayer we see in the life of Jesus.

*So much as we may know
with certainty from all the Gospels
tell of Jesus, that His prayer never was
merely a state of soul attained by some
sure method, an oratorio mentalis, a Prayer
of Quiet, a meditation, but an intercourse
and conversation with the heavenly Father,
an outlet for anguish and uncertainty and for
questions that needed answers; the bursting
forth of a tone of jubilation, a trembling yet
confident intimacy longing for undisturbed
intercourse with the Father in Heaven,
although the feeling of nearness and
fellowship with Him was wont
never to cease during the duties
and occupations of the day.*
—NATHAN SODERBLOM

In this kind of heartfelt prayer, we are drawn into an ever-deepening relationship with the One to whom we address our prayers.

The Lord is near to all who call on him,
to all who call on him in truth.
—PSALM 145:18

Come near to God,
and he will come near to you.
—JAMES 4:8

He prays well who is so absorbed with God
that he does not know he is praying.
—FRANCIS DE SALES

Prayer oneth the soul to God.
—JULIAN Of NORWICH

*Unless we are ready
to surrender ourselves to the
divine fire and to become that
burning bush of the desert which
burned and was never consumed,
we shall be scorched, because the
experience of prayer can only be
known from the inside and it
is not to be dallied with.*
—ANTHONY Of SOUROZH

The end result of such prayer is friendship with God, a treasure beyond anything this world can offer to us.

*"O God," I said, and that
was all. But what are the prayers
of the whole universe more than
expansions of that one cry? It is
not what God can give us,
but God that we want.*
—GEORGE MACDONALD

*In order that love be true
and the friendship endure, the wills
of the friends must be in accord....And
if you do not yet love him as He loves
you...you will endure this pain of spending
a long while with one who is so different
from you, when you see how much it
benefits you to possess His friendship
and how much He loves you....
Oh, what a good friend
You make, my Lord!*
—TERESA OF AVILA

*Contemplative prayer is
for those who are discontented with
second-hand descriptions of God, and
who want to experience the intimate
presence of God for themselves.*
—JAMES HOUSTON

*After I enter the chapel
I place myself in the presence of
God and I say to Him, "Lord, here
I am; give me whatever You wish." If He
gives me something, then I am happy and
I thank Him. If He does not give me anything,
then I thank Him nonetheless, knowing, as I do,
that I deserve nothing. Then I begin to tell Him
of all that concerns me, my joys, my thoughts,
my distress, and finally, I listen to Him.*
—CATHERINE LABOURÉ

*There is not in the world
a kind of life more sweet and
delightful than that of a continual
conversation with God.*
— BROTHER LAWRENCE

*It is no use to ask what
those who love God do with Him.
There is no difficulty in spending our
time with a friend we love; our heart is
always ready to open to Him; we do not
study what we shall say to Him, but
it comes forth without premeditation;
we can keep nothing back—even if
we have nothing special to say,
we like to be with Him.*
— FRANÇOIS FÉNELON

*Contact with Him is not
our achievement. It is a gift,
coming down to us from on high like a
meteor, rather than rising up like a rocket.
Before the words of prayer come to the lips,
the mind must believe in God's willingness
to draw near to us, and in our ability to
clear the path for His approach.
Such belief is the idea that
leads us toward prayer.*
—ABRAHAM HESCHEL

*There is none on earth that live
such a life of joy and blessedness as
those that are acquainted with this
heavenly conversation.*
—RICHARD BAXTER

And so we can celebrate that in prayer God draws close to us.

Come, 0 thou traveller unknown,
Whom still I hold but cannot see!
My company before is gone,
And I am left alone with thee.
With thee all night I mean to stay,
And wrestle till the break of day....
My prayer hath power with God.
His grace unspeakable I now receive:
Through faith I see thee face to face—
I see thee face to face, and live!
—CHARLES WESLEY

We talk about heaven being so
far away. It is within speaking distance
to those who belong there.
—DWIGHT L. MOODY

O Lord,
we know you love us.
you have demonstrated this in so many ways.
you have shown us your love in creating us
as unique receivers of your graces.
you have shown us your love
in giving us your son.
you have shown us your love in desiring
to transform us into your image.
you have shown us your love
in attending to our prayers.
we love you, Lord.
we desire your presence,
And come to you in all our faithlessness,
Thankful that you are willing to meet us there.
Amen.

-7-
TAKING UP THE CHALLENGE

The pages of this book have been filled with insights on prayer, testimonies of its effectiveness, and suggested methods that we might use to improve our prayer lives. Some of these methods and ideas might be new to you, and you may be excited about the prospect of putting them into practice. But if you approach the task with the expectation that the difficulties of prayer will be solved by learning a new technique or gaining a new perception, you will most likely be disappointed. Prayer is hard work. There is no easy shortcut to vibrant prayer.

Disappointment can also arise from thinking that every method will work for every person. But not every insight will be fruitful to every believer. Prayer is individual; as individual as your own personal relationship with God. What was helpful to one of the great writers of the past may be ineffective, unworkable, or impractical for you, no matter how much effort you expend. What is inspiring and eye-opening to one may be confusing to another. God made each of us unique, and His ways with us will be as individual as we are.

Find the way of prayer that works best for you. Often the most natural way of praying will be the best. For example, my knees tend to wear out pretty quickly, so I have found that a bracing walk outdoors creates, for me, a natural environment for prayer.

But just because it is natural or easy doesn't necessarily mean it is the best path. After all, we cannot allow ourselves to become lazy when it comes to spiritual matters. It would be a mistake to let your prayers be limited by your preferences or your natural tendencies. It is a good thing to break out of your accustomed mold. By the same token, don't always be searching for some new wrinkle or method. At its heart, prayer is a simple act. Don't muddy the waters by a search for the novel or the offbeat.

One of the best ways to improve your prayer life is by learning more about the focus of your prayers: God. Read the Scriptures to gain greater understanding of who God is and what He has done for us. Let your thinking about life be shaped by biblical truths, and consequently, your prayers as well. Our prayer lives are often limited or thrown off course by poor theological understanding, but they can be set afire when we gain deeper understanding about God's ways. If we seek God with our minds as well as our hearts, new vistas of understanding will open before us and more focus will be given to our prayers.

As I look back over the pages of this book I am reminded again of the relevance of the writings of the past for those of us who live in the present. There is much we can learn if we will bend our ears to the insights of the great saints who have preceded us. They challenge us anew not to take lightly the serious task of prayer.

But what should we do with the insights we have gained? If they remain only interesting concepts, if they do not penetrate into our hearts and challenge us, then they have failed to do their work. As Andrew Murray reminds us, prayer is something we learn by doing:

Reading a book about prayer,
listening to lectures and talking about it
is very good, but it won't teach you to pray.
You get nothing without exercise, without practice.
I might listen for a year to a professor of music
playing the most beautiful music, but that
won't teach me to play an instrument.

Hopefully, the profound thoughts about prayer recorded in this book will help us make the choice to give ourselves to prayer, for prayer begins with a choice: We must choose to involve God in all the various aspects of our life. We won't really begin to make progress in prayer until we decide to take prayer seriously. We may need to do some rearranging of our priorities. Prayer should be one of the major priorities in the life of the believer. Sadly, it often is crowded out by the press of other activities, even our "religious" ones.

When we look into the lives of these great men and women of the past we see a commitment to prayer. In fact, the strength and unflagging persistence of their prayer lives were such that they sometimes were referred to as the "athletes of prayer." In the same way that an athlete will structure his or her life around the accomplishment of a desired athletic goal—running faster, hitting the ball farther, developing greater endurance, and so on—so did these athletes of prayer make prayer central to their lives. They expended themselves to become better, and more fervent, prayers. By doing so, they changed the world.

Are we willing to do the same? Are we willing to restructure our goals, our priorities, and our time around the act of serious prayer? Will we expend the necessary energy to work at becoming more focused in our prayers? Will we make times of prayer a central part of our schedule rather than something we do if we can find the extra time? Are we willing to keep on practicing, to keep on praying, even when it becomes difficult, boring, seems pointless, or seems too emotionally demanding?

All the rich and profound thoughts on prayer, which we have as a legacy from the past, are no good to us unless they actually cause us to take prayer more seriously.

And we should take prayer seriously.

Any way we look at it, prayer is an awesome privilege. To think that the creator of all things desires to hear about all our little needs and concerns is a staggering thought. Seen from an eternal perspective, the matters that concern us are, for the most part, rather trivial. Who are we that God should bother to hear us? And yet, God does not hold our concerns to be trivial. The wonder of it all is that God is willing to concern Himself with what concerns us. That He is willing, and in fact desirous, of lending an ear to our problems and struggles reveals a great deal about our relationship with Him and His love for us.

Love is God's motivation for giving us the gift of prayer. It should also be our prime motivation in praying. We do not pray primarily to receive whatever it is we think we need, or to fulfill what we perceive to be our religious duty. We pray because we love God. We pray because our hearts cry out their need to communicate with Him. We pray because we desire His companionship with us on the pathway of life.

God is not an impersonal metaphysical force or an indifferent "supreme being." He has revealed Himself to be a lover—one who wants to be in relationship with His creatures. He is the source of all life and the giver of every good gift, even those gifts that may not seem good to us at the time we receive them. He is infinite, but He is also personal.

Prayer is the most intimate activity we can share with God. I do not think it is too much of a stretch to suggest that prayer is to our relationship with God what the sexual relationship is to a healthy marriage. It is the utmost in self-revelation, where we bare our hearts before God. In prayer we reveal our true selves and make ourselves vulnerable to God. We spend our passion in pursuing His pleasure. We long for His presence with us and in us.

As we undertake the life of prayer, then, it is important that we keep our eyes on what really matters. We should focus not on the methods of prayer, but on the One to whom we pray. A heart that pants for God as a deer pants for water (Psalm 42:1) is the foundation of true prayer. We pray because we long to be in communication with God. We want to speak, to pour out our hearts, to be heard. The glory of prayer is that we can be, in a sense, face to face with God, even as Adam was in the garden when God walked with him "in the cool of the day." Prayer truly is the pathway to the very heart of God!

Brief Biographies of Quoted Writers

AMBROSE (c. 340–397) Bishop, skilled orator, a profound influence on Augustine.

LANCELOT ANDREWES (1555–1626) Anglican churchman and one of the translators of the King James Version of the Bible.

AUGUSTINE (345–430) Early African bishop and prolific writer.

KARL BARTH (1886–1968) Swiss theologian.

RICHARD BAXTER (1615–1691) Puritan minister and prolific writer.

NICHOLAS BERDYAEV (1874–1948) Russian philosopher and theologian.

GEORGES BERNANOS (1888–1948) French novelist and spiritual writer.

DONALD BLOESCH (1928–   ) American theologian.

E. M. BOUNDS (1835–1913) Popular writer of many books on prayer.

PHILLIPS BROOKS (1835–1893) American minister and hymn writer.

JOHN BUNYAN (1628–1688) English writer of *Pilgrim's Progress* and other books.

GEORGE BUTTRICK (1892–1980) Anglo-American pastor and devotional writer.

JOHN CALVIN (1509–1564) French reformer and systematic theologian.

ADAM CLARKE (1762–1832) Methodist theologian and commentator.

CLEMENT OF ALEXANDRIA (c. 150–215) Early church writer and philosopher.

DEMETRIUS OF ROSTOV (died 232) Alexandrian bishop.

EMILY DICKINSON (1830–1886) American poet.

JACQUES ELLUL (1912–   ) French theologian and sociologist.

FRANÇOIS FÉNELON (1651–1715) French mystical writer.

CHARLES G. FINNEY (1792–1875) American evangelist and writer.

P. T. FORSYTH (1848–1921) Scottish theologian and writer.

FRANCIS DE SALES (1517–1622) Bishop of Geneva and mystical writer.

THOMAS GOODWIN (1600–1680) English reformed theologian.

GREGORY OF NYSSA (331–394) Influential church leader and pope.

MADAME GUYON (1648–1717) French mystic, founder of Quietist movement.

J. EDWIN HARTILL (1909–1981) American Bible teacher and speaker.

GEORGE HERBERT (1593–1633) English poet and pastor.

ABRAHAM HESCHEL (1907–1972) Orthodox Jewish theologian.

WALTER HILTON (died 1396) English mystical writer.

JAMES HOUSTON (1922–   ) English scholar and devotional writer.

E. STANLEY JONES (1884–1973) American missionary to India.

JULIAN OF NORWICH (c. 1342–1413) English mystical writer.

SÖREN KIERKEGAARD (1813–1855) Danish philosopher and theologian.

JOHN KNOX (1515–1572) Leader of the Scottish reformation and founder of the Church of Scotland.

CATHERINE LABOURÉ (1806–1876) French nun.

BROTHER LAWRENCE (c. 1605–1691) Monk and mystical writer.

C. S. LEWIS (1898–1963) English professor, prolific writer, and Christian apologist.

ABRAHAM LINCOLN (1809–1865) Sixteenth president of the United States.

MARTIN LUTHER (1483–1546) German founder of the Reformation, author of numerous treatises, commentaries, and devotional books.

GEORGE MACDONALD (1824–1905) Scottish minister, novelist, and poet.

THOMAS MERTON (1915–1968) American monk and mystical writer.

DWIGHT L. MOODY (1837–1889) American preacher and evangelist.

GEORGE MUELLER (1805–1898) German philanthropist, founder of numerous orphanages in Britain.

ANDREW MURRAY (1828–1917) South African devotional writer

PHILIP NERI (1515–1595) Italian church reformer.

JOHN HENRY NEWMAN (1801–1890) English scholar and theologian.

NOVALIS (1772–1801) German romantic poet.

ORIGEN (c. 185–254) Important early church theologian from Alexandria.

BLAISE PASCAL (1623–1662) Innovative scientist, philosopher, author of *Pensees* and an unfinished work of apologetics.

J. C. RYLE (1816–1900) English bishop and writer.

AUGUSTE SABATIER (1839–1901) French scholar and theologian.

W. E. SANGSTER (1900–1960) English preacher and scholar.

ANGELUS SILESIUS (1624–1677) Polish hymn writer.

NATHAN SODERBLOM (1866–1931) Swedish church leader and Nobel prize winner.

CHARLES SPURGEON (1834–1892) Gifted English preacher and writer.

J. HUDSON TAYLOR (1832–1905) English missionary pioneer.

JEREMY TAYLOR (1613–1667) English bishop and writer.

WILLIAM TEMPLE (1881–1944) Archbishop of Canterbury and prolific writer.

ALFRED LORD TENNYSON (1809–1892) English poet.

TERESA OF AVILA (1515–1592) Spanish mystic, writer, and church reformer.

TERTULLIAN (c. 160–230) Early church theologian.

THEOPHAN THE RECLUSE (1815–1894) Eastern Orthodox bishop and scholar.

THERESE DE LISIEUX (1873–1897) French Carmelite nun.

HELMUT THIELICKE (1908–) German theologian and preacher.

R. C. TRENCH (1807–1886) English theologian and church leader.

HENRY VAUGHN (1621–1695) English poet.

JOHN VIANNEY (1786–1859) French priest.

THOMAS WATSON (c. 1686) English theologian and preacher.

CHARLES WESLEY (1707–1788) Methodist reformer and hymn writer, brother to John.

JOHN WESLEY (1703–1791) Founder of Methodism.

ALEXANDER WHYTE (1836–1921) Influential British pastor and writer.

Samuel M. Zwemer (1867–1952) Dutch reformed
missionary.

Terry Glaspey is an editor and an author of several significant books, including *Your Child's Heart, Not a Tame Lion: The Spiritual Legacy of C. S. Lewis,* and *Great Books of the Christian Tradition.* He lives in Eugene Oregon.